Janet Wil

D0859859

MINE THE HARVEST

Books by

EDNA ST. VINCENT MILLAY

POEMS

The Buck in the Snow
Second April
Renascence
A Few Figs from Thistles
The Harp-weaver
Poems Selected for Young People
Fatal Interview
Wine from These Grapes
Conversation at Midnight
Huntsman, What Quarry?
Make Bright the Arrows
The Murder of Lidice
Collected Sonnets
Collected Lyrics
Mine the Harvest

PLAYS

The King's Henchman
The Lamp and the Bell
Aria da Capo
Three Plays
The Princess Marries the Page

Letters of Edna St. Vincent Millay,
edited by Allan Ross Macdougall

Mine the Harvest

A COLLECTION OF NEW POEMS

EDNA ST. VINCENT MILLAY

HARPER & BROTHERS *Publishers*
NEW YORK

MINE THE HARVEST

Copyright, *1945, 1946, 1947, 1952, 1953, 1954,*
by Norma Millay Ellis
Copyright, *1941, by Edna St. Vincent Millay*
Copyright, *1949, by Curtis Publishing Company*
Printed in the United States of America
All rights in this book are reserved.
No part of the book may be used or reproduced
in any manner whatsoever without written per-
mission except in the case of brief quotations
embodied in critical articles and reviews. For
information address Harper & Brothers
49 East 33rd Street, New York 16, N. Y.

SECOND EDITION

C-D

Library of Congress catalog card number: 54-6290

FOREWORD

AT THE time of her death in 1950, Edna St. Vincent
Millay was bringing together material for a new book of
poems. Many were already selected for the edition, although some had not yet been given titles. Several had
appeared in periodicals; many she had read to friends.
She was in correspondence with her publishers over pre-
liminary plans for the book. It is my genuine concern
that the character of this volume reflect such planning,
and I hesitate to intrude even here upon it. In both
content and arrangement it follows her own wishes and
practices as closely as possible.

Yet in fairness to such a careful editor as my sister,
it is also necessary to remind the reader that this edition
is a "collection" of her poems; and since she did not
live to fulfill her own plans for its publication, it is of
necessity an "edited" book. It has been my responsibility
to decide, in cases where the poet's own intentions remain in doubt, questions of selection, arrangement, and,
in a few instances, of alternative versions. The collection
is largely comprised of work produced since 1939. Included here also are several poems written at various
times during the poet's life which, for reasons of her
own, she withheld for later publication. The poem
"Journal," which comprises Part IV, is from an earlier

period. Some of the poems have been taken from the poet's working notebooks, where it was her custom to leave poems, after their original composition, for further reflection, though these often represented completed work. In two instances, namely poems beginning "See where the bittersweet" and "For whom the house of Montagu was neighbour," poems which gave some evidence of being incomplete have seemed of sufficient integrity and interest to be included. Although the poems under the title "Tristan" are complete in themselves, it is possible that they may not represent the extent of the poet's plan for this sequence; they had not been brought together; only one had been typed; also, sonnets numbers eighteen and nineteen being irregular in form it may have been her intention to indicate this, as she has done previously with deviations from the conventional sonnet. In those few instances where the choice between alternative readings, usually of single words, were not indicated by the poet, I have endeavored to carry out to the best of my understanding what might have been her decision.

The only word in this book not contributed by its author is the heading "Steepletop," under which three short poems that belong together are placed. Knowing full well my sister's feeling about alterations of her poems by anyone besides herself, I could present this book only in the sincere conviction that it contains the poetry of which she once reminded her editor "the faults as well as the virtues are my own."

Relating to this book: my gratitude to Cass Canfield and the Editorial Department of Harper & Brothers for their generous assistance; to Frances Park for her understanding work with me on the notebooks; and to John Christie, of the English Department of Vassar College, and Dorothy Sexton Christie, of the Vassar faculty, for their constant interest whatever the hour, and for their invaluable counsel whatever the problem.

NORMA MILLAY

Steepletop
January, 1954

CONTENTS

x

PART ONE

SMALL HANDS, RELINQUISH ALL

SMALL HANDS, relinquish all:
Nothing the fist can hold,—
Not power, not love, not gold—
But suffers from the cold,
And is about to fall.

The mind, at length bereft
Of thinking, and its pain,
Will soon disperse again,
And nothing will remain:
No, not a thought be left.

Exhort the closing eye,
Urge the resisting ear,
To say, "The thrush is here";
To say, "His song is clear";
To live, before it die.

Small hands, relinquish all:
Nothing the fist can hold,

Not power, not love, not gold,
But suffers from the cold,
And is about to fall.

The mind at length bereft
Of thinking and its pain,
Will soon disperse again,
And nothing will remain:
No, not a thing be left.

Only the ardent eye,
Only the listening ear
Can say, "The thrush was here!"
Can say, "His song was clear!"
Can live, before it die.

2

RAGGED ISLAND

THERE, THERE where those black spruces crowd
To the edge of the precipitous cliff,
Above your boat, under the eastern wall of the island;
And no wave breaks; as if
All had been done, and long ago, that needed
Doing; and the cold tide, unimpeded
By shoal or shelving ledge, moves up and down,
Instead of in and out;
And there is no driftwood there, because there is no
      beach;
Clean cliff going down as deep as clear water can reach;

No driftwood, such as abounds on the roaring shingle,
To be hefted home, for fires in the kitchen stove;
Barrels, banged ashore about the boiling outer harbor;
Lobster-buoys, on the eel-grass of the sheltered cove:

There, thought unbraids itself, and the mind becomes
      single.

There you row with tranquil oars, and the ocean
Shows no scar from the cutting of your placid keel;
Care becomes senseless there; pride and promotion
Remote; you only look; you scarcely feel.

Even adventure, with its vital uses,
Is aimless ardor now; and thrift is waste.

Oh, to be there, under the silent spruces,
Where the wide, quiet evening darkens without haste
Over a sea with death acquainted, yet forever chaste.

3

To WHOM the house of Montagu
Was neighbour, and that orchard near
Wherein all pleasant fruit-trees grew
Whose tops were silvered by the clear
Light of the blessèd, sworn-by moon,
(Or all-but-sworn-by—save that She,
Knowing the moon's inconstancy,
Dreaded that Love might change as soon. . . .
Which changèd never; or did change
Into something rich and strange);
To whom in infancy the sight
Of Sancho Panza and his Knight,
In noble, sad and awkward state
Approaching through the picket-gate,
Was warmer with the flesh of life
Than visits from the vicar's wife;
For whom from earliest days the lips
Of Her who launched the thousand ships
Curved in entrancing speech, and Troy
Was hurt by no historic boy,
But one more close and less a fool
Than boys who yanked your curls at school

(Far less a fool than he who lay
With willing Venus on a bed
Of anise, parsley, dill and rue,
A bank whereon the wild thyme grew,
And longed but to be gone from thence,—
Whom vainly Venus did implore
To do her that sweet violence
All boys and girls with any sense
Would die to do; but where she lay
Left her, and rose and rushed away
To stalk the tusky, small-eyed boar
He might have stalked another day);
And naked long Leander swam
The Thames, the Avon and the Cam,
And wet and chattering, white and cold
Appeared upon the pure threshold
Of Hero, whom the sight did move
To fear, to pity, and to love;

For such a child the peopled time,
When any man in any wood
Was shaggy like a goat, and stood
On hooves, and used his lusty strength
To blow through straws of different length
Bound all together; or could ride
A horse he never need bestride—

For such a child, that distant time
Was close as apple-trees to climb,
And apples crashed among the trees
Half Baldwin, half Hesperides.

4

THIS
Is mine, and I can hold it;
Lying here
In the hour before dawn, knowing that
 the cruel June
Frost has made the green lawn
White and brittle, smelling that the night
 was very cold,
Wondering if the lush, well-loved,
 well-tended,
Hoed and rowed and watched with pride
And with anxiety
So long,—oh, cruel, cruel,
Unseasonable June—
Whether all that green will be black
 long before noon—

This
I know: that what I hear
Is a thrush; and very near,
Almost on the sill of my open window,
 close to my ear.

I was startled, but I made no motion,
    I knew
What I had to do—stop breathing,
    not be
Here at all, and I have accomplished
    this. He has not yet known
Anything about me; he is singing very loud
And with leisure: he is all alone.

Oh, beautiful, oh, beautiful,
Oh, the most beautiful that I ever have
    heard,
Anywhere, including the nightingale.
It is not so much the tune
Although the tune is lovely, going
    suddenly higher
Than you expect, and neat, and
    something like the nightingale
    dropping
And throbbing very low.
It is not so much the notes, it is the
    quality of the voice,
Something to do perhaps with
    over-tone
And under-tone, and implication
Felt, but not quite heard—

Oh, this is much to ask
Of two delicate ear-drums and of some other
    perception
Which I do not understand, a little over-
    sensitive
Perhaps to certain sounds.
All my senses
Have broken their dikes and flooded
    into one, the sense of hearing.

I have no choice,
I think, if I wish to continue to live:
    I am beginning to shiver
Already; I may be shattered
Like a vessel too thin
For certain vibrations.
Go away now, I think; go down to the
    damp hemlocks near the brook
    in the hollow,
Where I cannot quite follow
Your deepest notes, through the dissipating
    air.
But return soon.

Not so soon, though,
Quite, perhaps,
As tomorrow.

5

Of what importance, O my lovely girls, my dancers,
    O my lovely boys,
My lovers and my dancers, and my lovely girls, my
    lovers and my dancers,
In a world so loud
Is our sweet noise?

Who is so proud
Of deftness in the ordered dance or on the ever-listening
    strings
Or of skill about the ankles with no rudeness the fine
    Tyrian folds
Arranging with such art that none beholds, or when she
    sings
Her songs by Aphrodite not unheard, so proud as I?—
(Who on this day, not unequipped with garlands pleas-
    ing to the gods, my lyre and my stylus, my stylus
    and my life put by!)

Go now to Gorgo, you, and learn from her
What dancing is and how 'tis done;

But cut for me, if ever you loved me, and you did, from
    your sweet-smelling curls
One each, from each one one,—
For I have a death to die which I may not defer—

And lay on the grave of what I may not live with
    and sleep well
Your pretty ringlets, O my pretty girls!—

How long my song must slumber, we shall see, or may
    not ever see—
No one can tell,
This is, I think, the serious death of me.

I die, that the sweet tongue of bound Aeolia never from
    her throat be torn, that Mitylene may be free
To sing, long after me.

Phaon, I shall not die for you again.
There are few poets. And my own child tells me there
    are other men.
Such poets as henceforth of their own will die, must die
    for more than you.
This I propose to do.

But die to no purpose? in full waste of body's brawn
    and skill and brain's instructed, rich and devious
    plot
To live?—not.

Death must be fertile, from this moment on, fertile, at
    least, as life.
For Man has all to lose: ordered and organized from this
    day on, must be his nightly
Watch, the locking of his shrine against defilers:
Skillful now indeed must be the thumbers of the record,
    the compilers:
Sharpened at all hours is the knife.

FEW COME this way; not that the darkness
Deters them, but they come
Reluctant here who fear to find,
Thickening the darkness, what they left behind
Sucking its cheeks before the fire at home,
The palsied Indecision from whose dancing head
Precipitately they fled, only to come again
Upon him here,
Clutching at the wrist of Venture with a cold
Hand, aiming to fall in with him, companion
Of the new as of the old.

THE STRAWBERRY SHRUB

STRAWBERRY SHRUB, old-fashioned, quaint as quinces,
Hard to find in a world where neon and noise
Have flattened the ends of the three more subtle senses;
And blare and magenta are all that a child enjoys.

More brown than red the bloom—it is a dense colour;
Colour of dried blood; colour of the key of F.
Tie it in your handkerchief, Dorcas, take it to school
To smell. But no, as I said, it is browner than red; it is
     duller
Than history, tinnier than algebra; and you are colour-
     deaf.

Purple, a little, the bloom, like musty chocolate;
Purpler than the purple avens of the wet fields;
But brown and red and hard and hiding its fragrance;
More like an herb it is: it is not exuberant.
You must bruise it a bit: it does not exude; it yields.

Clinker-built, the bloom, over-lapped its petals
Like clapboards; like a boat I had; like the feathers of
    a wing;
Not graceful, not at all Grecian, something from the
    provinces:
A chunky, ruddy, beautiful Boeotian thing.

Take it to school, knotted in your handkerchief, Dorcas,
Corner of your handkerchief, take it to school, and see
What your teacher says; show your pretty teacher the
    curious
Strawberry Shrub you took to school for me.

8

WHEN IT IS OVER

WHEN IT is over—for it will be over,
Though we who watched it be gone, watched it and
with it died—
Will there be none the less the yellow melilot, the white,
the high sweet clover,
Close to the dusty, fragrant, hot roadside?
Oh, yes, there will!—
Escaped from fields of fodder, for there must be fodder
still. . . .

Ah, yes, but nothing will escape . . .

Yet sweet, perhaps, in fields of fodder still.

When it is over—for it will be over—
Will there be none the less, will there be still
In April on the southern slope of an orchard, apple
orchard hill,
Red-and-white buds already fragrant, intent upon
blossoming?—
There will; I know there will.

But for whom will they blossom?—
                    They will blossom for what, not whom,
I think—the streakèd bloom
Red-and-white, and the hardy fragrance, strong, all but
    visible, almost but not quite in sight,
Long, long before its pretty petals in a May wind fall,
Will be the finished apple in the eyes of all beholding it;

I see him well: the human creature studying the only
    good
A tree can be—stout wood
For building or for pulp whereon to print the expedi-
    ent thing,
Or, if not that, food.
He walks through the apple orchard just now blossom-
    ing,
Dismissing to the necessary, the developing, past
The present beauty and the fragrance enfolding it.

9

The courage that my mother had
Went with her, and is with her still:
Rock from New England quarried;
Now granite in a granite hill.

The golden brooch my mother wore
She left behind for me to wear;
I have no thing I treasure more:
Yet, it is something I could spare.

Oh, if instead she'd left to me
The thing she took into the grave!—
That courage like a rock, which she
Has no more need of, and I have.

WILD-CAT, gnat and I
Go our ways under a grey sky.
Little that Himself has made
Ever finds me quite afraid . . .
Though if cat clawed me,
Gnat gnawed me,
I should shriek, or roll in grass,
Asking that this trouble pass.

Things that hunt in hunger
I stroke, across my fear:
Only anger
Brings the crashing tear.

11

THIS SHOULD be simple; if one's power were great,
If one were God, for instance,—and the world
Not yet created; Lucifer not hurled
Yet out of Heaven, to plot and instigate
Most thoughtful mischief: simple, in a state
Of non-existence, to manipulate
And mould unwieldy, heavy, obstinate
But thoughtless matter, into some bright world:—
Make something out of nothing, and create
As many planets, and as various men
And other mortal creatures as might seem
Consistent with the structure and the theme
Of one's proposed achievement; not from dream,
No, not from aspiration, not from hope,
But out of art and wisdom, and those powers
Such as must qualify a god, create
A world at least as beautiful and brave
And terrified and sorrowful as ours.

For nothingness is plastic, has no trend;
Is stubborn but in this: it is inert;

Wills not to render justice, nor do hurt;
And should be, in strong hands, easy to bend.

But evil upon evil laminate
Through layers uncountable as leaves in coal—
To strip that into strata—perpetrate
Such outrage upon evil; and create
Good out of wickedness at this late date—
There, there's a trick to tame the gamiest soul.

Sweet earth, you might from birth—oh beaming
    sight:—
With gentle glow have lighted all the night;
And Man, a star upon a planet, see,
Radiant beyond the furthest nebulae.

But earth, though grown to green and lush estate,
Her blossom, Man, has never yet unfurled:
Observe how bawdy, botched and profligate,
Except in greed, proceeds this pretty world.

We move in darkness solemn and extreme;
We falter forward, hesitate, decide
To turn about, pause, fumble, plunge, collide,—
Beg pardon, and then bob and bob about
From left to right,

Bump foreheads, then burst out
In nervous, merry laughter, and plunge forth
Into the forest suddenly, you running east by north,
Gasping and stumbling over stumps, and I
East by south,
Slashing through bogs, tripped by submerged logs and
     with muddy water in my mouth,
Till every sound subsides
And all is lost in darkness and in fog,
And neither of us has thought to say goodnight.

Such blindness does not intercept the sight
Of the efficient: they have learned by heart
By daylight, from a most meticulous chart
Just where to go; they know . . .
And can as well through darkness as by day
Find their direct, discreet, expedient way:
Know where to go to muster, or to hide;
They move among us all throughout the night;
They pass close by your side;
You do not hear their step, they step so light.

. . . why cannot we as well as they
Scout, reconnoiter, photograph, survey,
Make maps and study them, and learn our way?—
Or must we lie and sleep, "because 'tis night"?

Then it is true, that in this world today
Lucifer, alone, can bring men light.

Must double-dealing, like a snake's forked tongue,
Flick red at us from under every stone?
Must Honour be self-conscious, being alone?—
And Aspiration, an infected lung?

Must Justice always dawdle, don its wig,
And wipe its spectacles before it speaks?
And Government keep flapping to and fro
Like a loose shutter on a hinge that squeaks?—
Kindness of heart be such a whirligig?
Courtesy mince and bow with pointed toe?
Piety smirk?—and Scholarship repose
In camphor, saving on Commencement Day?

Evil alone has oil for every wheel;
Rolls without friction and arrives on time;
Looks forward and sees far; does not reveal
Itself in conversation; is sublime
In logic; is not wasteful; does not feel
Compunction; buries the dead past in lime.

I think, perhaps, the gods, who may not die,
May not achieve unconsciousness, forget

Even their errors or their sins, are set
On making daily pieties comply
With nightly assignations—and are shy
Of mortal things, like laughter, say, or tears,—
Things which they might regret an eon of years—
Fervour, devotion, fright, audacity.

But we are singled out,—oh, we have doom
To comfort us,—sweet peril, imminent death—
So we have leisure, we have time, have room
For wide despair and all its leagues beneath,
Lethal delights the gods dare not assume,
And, not possessing them, cannot bequeath.
And, out of haughty, smooth, serene despair,
We might envisage, and we might fulfill
Appointments and arrangements, which the fair
Soft gods have never made, and never will.

From so much energy, so little hope,
So vast a consolation in the end,
We could erect a thing of poise and scope,
Which future generations might defend,
And put to their own use; and what we grope
To get a glimpse of, they might comprehend.

To build a house would be, it seems to me,
An easy task, if you had solid, good,
Simple material, clean of history:
Honest, unbiased brick, cement, and wood—
If you had sense, authority, and time,
And need not quibble, shift, cajole, subdue,
Break down partitions, breathe old hair and lime,
And tease the out-of-plumb into the true—
If you need not, for instance, for one thing,
Lure ancient chimneys to be lined with tile,
Oh, what a joy! Oh, hear the hammers ring!
A house!—and building houses is worth while.

We, we, the living, we, the still-alive,—
Why, what a triumph, what a task is here!
But how to go about it?—how connive
To outwit Evil in his proper sphere
And element?—Evil, conservative,
Established, disciplined, adroit, severe.
And yet, in some way, yet, we may contrive
To build our world; if not this year, next year.

12

SONG

Beautiful Dove, come back to us in April:
You could not over-winter on our world.
Fly to some milder planet until springtime;
Return with olive in your claws upcurled.

Leave us to shrikes and ravens until springtime:
We let them find their food as best they may;
But you, we do not grow the grain you feed on;
And you will starve among us, if you stay.

But oh, in April, from some balmier climate
Come back to us, be with us in the spring!
If we can learn to grow the grain you feed on,
You might be happy here; might even sing.

PART TWO

1

NEW ENGLAND SPRING, 1942

THE RUSH of rain against the glass
Is louder than my noisy mind
Crying, "Alas!"

The rain shouts: "Hear me, how I melt the ice that
 clamps the bent and frozen grass!
Winter cannot come twice
Even this year!
I break it up; I make it water the roots of spring!
I am the harsh beginning, poured in torrents down the
 hills,
And dripping from the trees and soaking, later, and
 when the wind is still,
Into the roots of flowers, which your eyes, incredulous,
 soon will suddenly find!
Comfort is almost here."

The sap goes up the maple; it drips fast
From the tapped maple into the tin pail
Through tubes of hollow elder; the pails brim;
Birds with scarlet throats and yellow bellies sip from
 the pail's rim.

Snow falls thick; it is sifted
Through cracks about windows and under doors;
It is drifted through hedges into country roads. It cannot last.
Winter is past.
It is hurling back at us boasts of no avail.

But Spring is wise. Pale and with gentle eyes, one day
    somewhat she advances;
The next, with a flurry of snow into flake-filled skies
    retreats before the heat in our eyes, and the thing
    designed
By the sick and longing mind in its lonely fancies—
The sally which would force her and take her.
And Spring is kind.
Should she come running headlong in a wind-whipped
    acre
Of daffodil skirts down the mountain into this dark
    valley we would go blind.

2

HERE IN A ROCKY CUP

HERE IN a rocky cup of earth
The simple acorn brought to birth
What has in ages grown to be
A very oak, a mighty tree.
The granite of the rock is split
And crumbled by the girth of it.

Incautious was the rock to feed
The acorn's mouth; unwise indeed
Am I, upon whose stony heart
Fell softly down, sits quietly,
The seed of love's imperial tree
That soon may force my breast
    apart.

"I fear you not. I have no doubt
My meagre soil shall starve you
    out!"

Unless indeed you prove to be
The kernel of a kingly tree;
Which if you be I am content
To go the way the granite went,
And be myself no more at all,
So you but prosper and grow tall.

How INNOCENT we lie among
The righteous!—Lord, how sweet we smell,
Doing this wicked thing, this love,
Bought up by bishops!—doing well,
With all our leisure, all our pride,
What's illy done and done in haste
By licensed folk on every side,
Spitting out fruit before they taste.

(That stalk must thrust a clubby bud;
Push an abortive flower to birth.)

Under the moon and the lit scud
Of the clouds, the cool conniving earth
Pillows my head, where your head lies;

Weep, if you must, into my hair
Tomorrow's trouble: the cold eyes
That know you gone and wonder where.

But tell the bishops with their sons,
Shout to the City Hall how we
Under a thick barrage of guns
Filched their divine commodity.

ARMENONVILLE

By THE lake at Armenonville in the Bois de Boulogne
Small begonias had been set in the embankment, both
   pink and red;
With polished leaf and brittle, juicy stem;
They covered the embankment; there were wagon-loads
   of them,
Charming and neat, gay colors in the warm shade.

We had preferred a table near the lake, half out of view,
Well out of hearing, for a voice not raised above
A low, impassioned question and its low reply.
We both leaned forward with our elbows on the table,
   and you
Watched my mouth while I answered, and it made me
   shy.
I looked about, but the waiters knew we were in love,
And matter-of-factly left us blissfully alone.

There swam across the lake, as I looked aside, avoiding
Your eyes for a moment, there swam from under the
   pink and red begonias

*

A small creature; I thought it was a water-rat; it swam
    very well,
In complete silence, and making no ripples at all
Hardly; and when suddenly I turned again to you,
Aware that you were speaking, and perhaps had been
    speaking for some time,
I was aghast at my absence, for truly I did not know
Whether you had been asking or telling.

5

TRISTAN

I

PUT IT down! I say; put it down,—here, give it to me,
    I know what is in it, you Irish believer in fairies!
    Here, let me smash it
Once and for all,
Against the corner of the wall!
Do we need philtres?

Look at me! Look at me! Then come here.
This fearful thing is pure
That is between us. I want to be sure that nothing
    drowses it. Look at me!
This torture and this rapture will endure.

I STILL can see
How you hastily and abstractedly flung down
To the floor,
Having raked it, arm after arm,
Over your head,
Your lustrous gown;
And how, before
Its silken susurration had subsided,
We were as close together as it is possible
    for two people to be.

It was your maid, I think,
Who picked it up in the morning, while we lay
Still abed, exhausted by inexhaustible love;
I saw her, I saw her through half-closed eyes,
    kneel above it,
And smooth it, with a concerned hand, and a face
    full of thoughtfulness.
Not that the dress
Was fragile,
Or had suffered harm,
But that you had planned
To walk in it, when you walked ashore;
And our ship was getting minute by minute,
    more and more
Close to Tintagel.

THERE WERE herbs strown
Over the bed-room floor, alkanet,
Perhaps, and several of the mints, and costmary,
Too, I think; they were fresh and brash and fragrant,
    but a man can forget
All names but one. I was not alone in the room.
Even in the morning they were fresh, they had not
    died.
We had meant to have tied
Some of them into garlands, but we had no time.
They were fragrant even without being touched, there
    was so much
Pressure against them from the passion that beat against
    that room
Enough to wrench its rafters down.
I was late getting down
To the shore. Women there,
With sea-wind slashing their hair into their eyes, were
    drying
Long net and long net and long net.

4

HEAVILY ON the faithful bulk of Kurvenal,
My servant for a long time, leaning,
With footsteps less from weakness than for pleasure
    in the green grass, lagging, I came here,
Out of the house, to lie, propped up on pillows, under
    this fine tree—
Oak older than I, but still, not being ill, growing,
Granted to feel, I think, barring lightning, year after
    year,—and barring the axe—
For a long time yet, the green sap flowing.

6

DREAM OF SABA

CALM WAS Half-Moon Bay; we lay at anchor there
Just off Tortola; when the hurricane,
Leaving its charted path, leapt full upon us,
And we were bruised and sobbing from the blows of the
    rain
Before we knew by what we were attacked or could in
    any way prepare.

"How dark it is tonight!" someone had said.
The lantern in the rigging burned serene
Through its glass chimney without crack and polished
    clean;
The wick well trimmed; plenty of kerosene.
We went to bed.

Following a fearful night I do not quite remember came
    a kind of dawn, not light,
But something we could see by. And we saw
What we had missed by inches; what we were headed
    for.

Astern, in an empty sea,
Suddenly, and before a man could cry, "Look there!"
Appeared what for an instant seemed to be
Black backs of half a hundred porpoises.
Before the eyes could blink at these,
They were black reefs, which rose into the air
With awful speed till they were mountains; these, one
    moment there,
Streaming sea-water stood against the sky;
Then all together and with awful speed diminished and
    like porpoises were gone,
Leaving the sea bare.

We turned from staring aft, and dead ahead, a mile
    away,
It seemed, through the thick steam of a white boiling
    surf and through smashed spray,
Saw the tall naked grooved precipitous sides and concave
    top
Of a volcanic island—its volcano now extinct,
It seemed; but it was hard to say.
From its high crater no red flame
Was seen to pulse and pour
But was it indeed or was it alone the steam from the
    burning breakers that kept us from seeing more?

There was no harbour. Those steep sides without a
    strand
Went down.
Yet even as from eye to brain this swift perception
    flashed, there seemed to reach
Even more swiftly toward us from that island now mirac-
    ulously in height and size increased
A broadening sandless beach
Humped with round boulders mossed with brightest
    green,
And purple with prostrate sea-ferns and stiff upright
    purple fans;
Red with anemones, and brilliant blue, and yellow dotted
    with black
From many fishes, lashing in the draining pools
Or sliding down the narrow sluices from the encroaching
    land to the receding sea.

The water thinned; we saw beneath us now
The bottom clearly; and from the vessel's bow
Saw close ahead, in shallow pool or dripping crevice
    caught,
The lovely fishes, rosy with azure fins or cobalt blue or
    yellow striped with black,
Curve their bright bodies double and lash forth and leap
    and then fall back with heavy splash
Or from the crevice leap and on the slippery weeds slide
    down once more into the narrow crack.

The thump and scrape of our keel upon the shore
Shook us from horror to a friendly sound!
Danger, maybe death, but decent, and the cause known.
Yet neither hook nor oar
Was overside before a Wave like a giant's palm
Was under us and raising us, gently, straight into the sky.
We rose beside the cliffs; we passed them so close by
We saw some little plants with reddish-purple flowers
Growing in a rock; and lying on a narrow ledge
Some birds' eggs; and some birds screamed at us as we
     passed.

The Wave did not break against the cliff; with utmost
     calm
It lifted us. The cliff had niches now where green grass
     grew.
And on a foot-high bush in a cleft some raspberries were
     ripe. And then at last
We saw the crater's edge.
The Wave curved over the rim and set us down in a
     cradle of branches, and withdrew.

It has not returned. Far down, the roaring of the sea
     abates
From hour to hour. The sky above our bowl is blue.

7

Who hurt you so,
My dear?
Who, long ago
When you were very young,
Did, said, became, was . . . something that you did not
    know
Beauty could ever do, say, be, become?—
So that your brown eyes filled
With tears they never, not to this day, have shed . . .
Not because one more boy stood hurt by life,
No: because something deathless had dropped dead—
An ugly, an indecent thing to do—
So that you stood and stared, with open mouth in which
    the tongue
Froze slowly backward toward its root,
As if it would not speak again, too badly stung
By memories thick as wasps about a nest invaded
To know if or if not you suffered pain.

8

WHEN THE tree-sparrows with no sound
    through the pearl-pale air
Of dawn, down the apple-branches, stair by stair,
With utmost, unforgettable, elegance and grace
Descended to the bare ground (never bare
Of small strewn seeds
For forced-down flyers at this
    treacherous time of year),
And richly and sweetly twittered there,
I pressed my forehead to the window,
    butting the cold glass
Till I feared it might break, disturbing the sparrows, so
    let the moment pass
When I had hoped to recapture the rapture of my dark
    dream;
I had heard as I awoke my own voice thinly scream,
"Where? in what street? (I knew the city) did they
    attack
You, bound for home?"
You were, of course, not there.
And I of course wept, remembering where I last had
    met you,

Yet clawed with desperate nails at the sliding dream,
  screaming not to lose, since I cannot forget you.
I felt the hot tears come;
Streaming with useless tears, which make the ears
  roar and the eyelids swell,
My blind face sought the window-sill
To cry on—frozen mourning melted
  by sly sleep,
Slapping hard-bought repose with quick successive blows
  until it whimper and outright weep.

The tide pulls twice a day,
The sunlit and the moonlit tides
Drag the rough ledge away
And bring back seaweed, little else besides.
Oh, do not weep these tears salter
  than the flung spray!—
Weepers are the sea's brides . . .
I mean this the drowning way.

PART THREE

1

Amorphous is the mind; its quality
Is in its fibre, not its form;
If it desire to fly it puts on wings,
Awkwardly, not like a bird
At first (though later); the rustle
    of a thing half-heard
Can twist it as iron at times
    is twisted by a wind-storm
    or word after word
Can pummel it for hours yet leave it
    like a leaf on a still day
    unstirred.

But a man's habit clings
And he will wear tomorrow
    what today he wears.

The mind is happy in the air,
    happy to be up there with
Learning feathers, but the man
    loathes it.

The mind cries "Up! Oh, up!
    Oh, let me try to fly!
Look! I can lift you!" but
    he smothers its cry;
Out of thrift, and fear of next year's
    feathers, he clothes it in last year's
    things
And tries his best to button across a keel-
    shaped breast a coat knobbed out
    by new wings.

2

FOR WARMTH ALONE, FOR SHELTER ONLY

For warmth alone, for shelter only
From the cold anger of the eyeless wind,
That knows my whereabouts, and mainly
To be at your door when I go down
Is abroad at all tonight in town,
I left my phrase in air, and sinned,
Laying my head against your arm
A moment, and as suddenly
Withdrawing it, and sitting there,
Warmed a little but far from warm,
And the wind still waiting at the foot of the stair,
And much harm done, and the phrase in air.

THE AGNOSTIC

The tired agnostic longs for prayer
More than the blest can ever do:
Between the chinks in his despair,
From out his forest he peeps through
Upon a clearing sunned so bright
He cups his eyeballs from its light.

He for himself who would decide
What thing is black, what thing is white,
Whirls with the whirling spectrum wide,
Runs with the running spectrum through
Red, orange, yellow, green and blue
And purple,—turns and stays his stride
Abruptly, reaching left and right
To catch all colours into light—
But light evades him: still he stands
With rainbows streaming through his hands.

He knows how half his hours are spent
In blue or purple discontent,
In red or yellow hate or fright,

And fresh young green whereon a blight
Sits down in orange overnight.

Yet worships still the ardent sod
For every ripped and ribboned hue,
For warmth of sun and breath of air,
And beauty met with everywhere;
Not knowing why, not knowing who
Pumps in his breath and sucks it out,
Nor unto whom his praise is due.

Yet naught nor nobody obeys
But his own heart, which bids him, "Praise!"
This, knowing that doubled were his days
Could he but rid his mind of doubt—
Yet will not rid him, in such ways
Of awful dalliance with despair—
And, though denying, not betrays.

THE APPLE-TREES bud, but I do not.
Who forgot
April?
Happiness, happiness, which
      once I held in my hand,
Does it persist?
Does it exist,
Perhaps, in some foreign land?

Did it expand
Somewhere into something that would
    twist my wrist?
Does it exist,
Sweeter than I could bear,
Anywhere?

*

There is no speed
In Indianapolis, or in
      Monte Carlo,
Which can exceed the awful
      speed of my thought.

These tiny Fiats and Bugattis
With the behind-them bespectacled
Looking like beetles, men who
    must go fast
In order to live, in order to
    outlast
Those that pile up on sand bags,
There is nothing so fast,
I find, as the motion of the mind.

*

Why did you, June, June,
So suddenly
Arrive at noon
In the midst of July?

I was not prepared
For the deferred appearance
Of your purple-haired
    adherence
To all that we live for.

What can I give for
Your knowledge
Of when to expand
And when to contract—

This instructed, more academic
    college
Of when to act?

*

Oh sovereign angel,
Wide winged stranger above a
    forgetful earth,
Care for me, care for me. Keep
    me unaware of danger
And not regretful
And not forgetful of my innocent
    birth.

If ever I should get warm
Again, which I somewhat doubt,
I shall light two candles,
One to St. Christopher
And one for me,
To keep us out
Of danger, and free from harm
In our adventurous voyage
Over cold
Unseen sea.

BLACK HAIR you'd say she had, or rather
Black crest, black nape and black lore-feather
Above the eye; eye black, and ring
About it white, white breast and wing;
Soft bill; (no predatory thing—
Three claws in front and one in back
But sparrow-fingered, for attack
Unfitted)—yet the questioning,
The desperate notes I did not hear,
Being pitched too high for human ear,
But seen so plainly in the eye
She turned upon me urgently
And watched me with as she went by
And close before me following,
Perching, and ever peering back,
Uttered, I know, some desperate cry,
I might have answered, had I heard:—
Ah, no; ah, no; poor female bird
With unmelodious throat and wing:
Sit on your eggs, by crimson king
Or gold made fertile; hatch them, bring
Beauty to birth, that it may sing

And leave you; be not haggard; cling
To what you have: a coloured thing
That grows more coloured every spring,
And whilst you warm his eggs, no lack
Will let you suffer: when they crack—
Feed them, and feed yourself; whilst he
Hangs from a thistle drunkenly,
Or loops his little flights between
The maple and the evergreen.
Utter your querulous chirp or quack;
And if his voice be anything,
Why, shut your lids and hear him sing,
And when he wants you, take him back.

6

CAVE CANEM

IMPORTUNED THROUGH the mails, accosted over the
   telephone, overtaken by running footsteps, caught
   by the sleeve, the servant of strangers,
While amidst the haste and confusion lover and friend
   quietly step into the unreachable past,
I throw bright time to chickens in an untidy yard.

Through foul timidity, through a gross indisposition to
   excite the ill-will of even the most negligible,
Disliking voices raised in anger, faces with no love in
   them,
I avoid the looming visitor,
Flee him adroitly around corners,
Hating him, wishing him well;

Lest if he confront me I be forced to say what is in no
   wise true:
That he is welcome; that I am unoccupied;
And forced to sit while the potted roses wilt in the crate
   or the sonnet cools
Bending a respectful nose above such dried philosophies

As have hung in wreaths from the rafters of my house
    since I was a child.

Some trace of kindliness in this, no doubt,
There may be.
But not enough to keep a bird alive.

There is a flaw amounting to a fissure
In such behaviour.

AN ANCIENT GESTURE

I THOUGHT, as I wiped my eyes on the corner of my
    apron:
Penelope did this too.
And more than once: you can't keep weaving all day
And undoing it all through the night;
Your arms get tired, and the back of your neck gets
    tight;
And along towards morning, when you think it will
    never be light,
And your husband has been gone, and you don't know
    where, for years,
Suddenly you burst into tears;
There is simply nothing else to do.

And I thought, as I wiped my eyes on the corner of my
    apron:
This is an ancient gesture, authentic, antique,
In the very best tradition, classic, Greek;
Ulysses did this too.
But only as a gesture,—a gesture which implied
To the assembled throng that he was much too moved
    to speak.
He learned it from Penelope . . .
Penelope, who really cried.

JESUS TO HIS DISCIPLES

I HAVE instructed you to follow me
What way I go;
The road is hard, and stony,—as I know;
Uphill it climbs, and from the crushing heat
No shelter will be found
Save in my shadow: wherefore follow me; the footprints
    of my feet
Will be distinct and clear;
However trodden on, they will not disappear.

And see ye not at last
How tall I am?—Even at noon I cast
A shadow like a forest far behind me on the ground.

9

ESTABLISHMENT IS shocked. Stir no adventure
Upon this splitted granite.

*

I will no longer connive
At my own destruction:—I will not again climb,
Breaking my finger nails, out of reach of the reaching
        wave,
To save
What I hope will still be me
When I have slid on slime and clutched at slippery
    rock-weed, and had my face towed under
In scrubbing pebbles, under the weight of the wave and
        its thunder.
I decline to scratch at this cliff. *If* is not a word.
I will connive no more
With that which hopes and plans that I shall not survive:
Let the tide keep its distance;
Or advance, and be split for a moment by a thing very
        small but all resistance;
Then do its own chore.

10

SOME THINGS ARE DARK

SOME THINGS are dark—or think they are.
But, in comparison to me,
All things are light enough to see
In any place, at any hour.

For I am Nightmare: where I fly,
Terror and rain stand in the sky
So thick, you could not tell them from
That blackness out of which you come.

So much for "where I fly": but when
I strike, and clutch in claw the brain—
Erebus, to such brain, will seem
The thin blue dusk of pleasant dream.

If it should rain—(the sneezy moon
Said: Rain)—then I shall hear it soon
From shingles into gutters fall . . .
And know of what concerns me, all:

The garden will be wet till noon—
I may not walk—my temper leans
To myths and legends—through the beans
Till they are dried—lest I should spread
Diseases they have never had.

I hear the rain: it comes down straight.
Now I can sleep, I need not wait
To close the windows anywhere.

Tomorrow, it may be, I might
Do things to set the whole world right.
There's nothing I can do tonight.

THE PARSI WOMAN

Beautiful Parsi woman in your pale silk veil
With the gold border, why do you watch the sky?
The sky is thick and cloudy with the bold strong wings
Of the vulture, that shall tear your breast and thigh,
On the tall Tower of Silence where you at length must
    lie.

Ah, but have not I,
I too at the end of the northern May
When the pasture slope was pink with the wild azalea
And fragrant with its breath,
Touched the brown treacherous earth with my living
    hand?—
Thrown me prone on my own green coffin-lid,
And smiled at the grass and had no thought of death?

You there with the tranquil lovely brow,
What do you see so high,—some beautiful thing?
The sun on the vulture's wing?

PART FOUR

JOURNAL

This book, when I am dead, will be
A little faint perfume of me.
People who knew me well will say,
"She really used to think that way."
I do not write it to survive
My mortal self, but, being alive
And full of curious thoughts today,
It pleases me, somehow, to say,
"This book when I am dead will be
A little faint perfume of me."

＊

Thoughts come so thickly to my head
These days, and will not be gainsaid,
Almost I think I am about
To end my thinking and pass out.
I have no heart to chide a thought
That with the careful blood is bought
Of one of my last moments here,
However barren it appear,—

Wherefore respectfully I write
Such dullness as I now indite.

*

That need is mine which comes to each:
To speak aloud in honest speech
What doubts and dogmas have confined
The shadowy acres of his mind.

*

If I, making my awkward way
Among my cluttered thoughts some day,
The lost and ominous key should find
To the sealed chamber of my mind,
Would I the secret room explore
And, knowing what I know, know more?

What fearful thing might not there be
Therein, to take away from me
The remnant of my little hour?—
Which, dark though it be, is not so dour
As in that chamber might be found;
Else should I now be underground.

It might be, now I think of it,
That such a key would nicely fit
The lock which Bluebeard set to prove

The patience of his ladies' love;
In which case, 'twould be fairly wise
To leave it lying where it lies.

*

Speaking of Bluebeard, might it be
The story is a pleasantry?—
What lovely fun! There in the vault
The obedient wives,—being those at fault—
While helped to half the kingdom she
Who had the sense to use the key!

(Maeterlinck had a web to weave
Across this legend, I believe;
But did not state his point so clearly
As I have done above, not nearly.
At least, that is to say, whatever
His point may be, said spicule never
Emerges far above the troubled
Face of the deep; if I have doubled
Upon him, as a consequence,
And gleaned away his general sense,
You can't blame *me*,—the wrong I do 'im
Is, as you might say, coming to 'im:
Who can't speak out in black and white
Deserves to lose his copyright.)

*

Why am I forever saying
Words I do not mean?—and laying
Ghosts of beauties that were dear,
With a laugh, or shrug, or sneer?
Does perhaps a balance stand
Between the Devil on one hand
And God on the other, which must be gained
As often as lost, and so maintained?—
And what I love as my own soul
I spit upon—to make me whole?

See, lest you grow too big for me,
Beauty, I prune your little tree!

*

I think that I would rather be
Blind than deaf; for frequently,
When birds were happy in the spring,
I've closed my eyes to hear them sing,
And felt the sun warm on my head,
And still could see some blue and red,
And all the things I ever saw
Remembered plain enough to draw.

But when, in order not to hear,
I've put a finger in each ear

At moments when I was a child,
The world stood still,—and I was wild!
'Twas like being chased in some bad dream;
Or silence following a scream.

I think that I could easily find
My way about, if I were blind.
Not in the city, it may be;
But in the woods, and by the sea.
No memory to my ear could teach
The sound of waves along the beach;
Though, hearing them, I could have guessed
The comb that curls along the crest,
And breaks and flattens and expands
Miraculously up the sands
In rapid-crawling sudsy water,
Like a white ink-stain through a blotter.

My sight, that was the activest
Of all the senses I possessed,
Would in its time have gathered most
For memory, if itself were lost.

Now, I could very easily tell
An apple-orchard by the smell,

And in my mind's eye see again
The rough bark blackened by the rain
And glistening, and the hardy big
Red and white blossoms on the twig.

But nothing could recall the sound
Of apples falling on the ground.
Though I should see an apple fall,
The sight of it could not recall
The sound. It would be like a stone
Into a bottomless cavern thrown,
That sends up no faint shout to tell
It reached the earth, and all is well.

I think if I should lose my eyes
My other senses all would rise
And walk beside me, bending down
To catch my brow's uncertain frown;
And when we came to something new
Or perilous to journey through,
Would lead me kindly by the hand;
And everyone would understand.

*

I do believe the most of me
Floats under water; and men see
Above the wave a jagged small

Mountain of ice, and that is all.
Only the depths of other peaks
May know my substance when it speaks,
And steadfast through the grinding jam
Remain aware of what I am.
Myself, I think, shall never know
How far beneath the wave I go.

*

What it would be like to die . . .
What it would be like to lie
Knowing nothing,—the keen mind
Suddenly gone deaf and blind;
Not even knowing that it knows
Nothing at all; one must suppose
That this mind, which in its day
Mused on the mysterious way
Of stars and cancers in their courses,
On heat and light and other forces,
And through its little eye could see
A section of infinity,
Is at last—and yet, not so!—
Is *not*—everything we know.
Is *not* here and *is not* there,
Is *not* earth and *is not* air,
Is *not* even a keen mind

Suddenly gone deaf and blind,
Is not any possible thing
Itself could be conjecturing;
Nor cherishes in a new TO-BE
Its little self's integrity.

Here at last the miracle!—
The hen squeezed back into the shell,
The man crushed back into the womb
Whose wall he burst,—and plenty of room!
DEATH!—how monstrously he comes—
Outside all nature's axioms!

"Dust to dust!"—oh, happier far
The ashes of my body are,
Since all that's mortal of me goes
The deathless way of dew and rose!
Year by year the wasted plain
Eats its death and lives again;
And the dusty body heaves
Its death aside and puts forth leaves.
The mind, that sees its errand, must
In truth desire itself were dust.

When by-which-I-came-to-be
Shall uncreate as deftly me,

Where my irrevelant ashes lie
Write only this: THAT WHICH WAS I
NO LONGER HOLDS ITS LITTLE PLACE
AGAINST THE PUSHING LEAGUES OF SPACE.

*

I read with varying degrees
Of bile the sage philosophies,
Since not a man has wit to purge
His pages of the Vital Urge.
At my head when I was young
Was Monad of all Monads flung;
And in my ears like any wind
Dubito Ergo Sum was dinned.
(When a chair was not a chair
Was when nobody else was there;
And Bergson's lump of sugar awed
My soul to see how slow it thawed!)

I, too, have mused upon the way
The sun comes up and makes the day,
The tide goes out and makes the shore,
And many, many matters more;
And coaxed till I was out of breath
My mind to take the hurdle, Death.
I, too, have writ my little book

On Things 'Twere Best to Overlook;
And struck a match and drawn a cork
And called a spade a salad-fork.
For men that are afraid to die
Must warm their hands before a lie;
The fire that's built of What is Known
Will chill the marrow in the bone.

Listen to a little story:
One day in a laboratory,
Where I was set to guess and grope,
I looked into a microscope.
I saw in perfect pattern sprawl
Something that was not there at all,
Something, perhaps, being utterly
Invisible to the naked eye,
By Descartes' doubt as all untrod
As furrows in the brain of God.
If, now, the naked eye can see
So little of the chemistry
By which itself is hale or blind,—
What, then, about the naked mind?

Think you a brain like as two peas
To any chattering chimpanzee's,
As 'twere a nut in the cheek shall nurse

The riddle of the universe?

Have we no patience, pray, to wait
Until that somewhat out-of-date,
Unwieldy instrument, the mind,
Shall be re-modeled and refined?
Or must we still abuse and vex
Our darkness with the Vital X,
Straining, with nothing given, to scan
The old equation: What is Man?

The sage philosopher at night,
When other men are breathing light,
Out of a troubled sleep I see
Start up in bed, holding the key!—
And wrap him in his dressing-gown,
And get him up and set him down,
And write enough to ease his head,
And rub his hands, and go to bed;—
And at the window, peering through,
All this time—the Bugaboo!

*

I know a better way to spend
An hour, than itching on its end.
'Tis not, as peevish Omar sang,
To swill, and let the world go hang.

But tenderly and with high mirth
To hang up garlands on the earth,
Nor chide too much the generous whim
That sensed a god and honored him.

Whether the moon be made of cheese,
Or eaten out by some disease,
And be the earth at center hot,
But cooling in, or be it not,
This fact holds true: the mind of man
Is desolate since its day began,
Divining more than it is able
To measure with its tiny table.

Oh, children, growing up to be
Adventurers into sophistry,
Forbear, forbear to be of those
That read the root to learn the rose;
Whose thoughts are like a tugging kite,
Anchored by day, drawn in at night.

Grieve not if from the mind be loosed
A wing that comes not home to roost;
There may be garnered yet of that
An olive-branch from Ararat.

*

I was so afraid to die,
I walked in ague under the sky.
As sure as I fared forth alone,
There fell Death's shadow beside my own,
There hung his whisper at my ear:
"Now I'm here!—But now I'm here!"

Thus his swift and terrible ways
Were mildew on my living days,
And Death forbore to carry off
A wretch already dead enough.

I heard him in the heavy sound
Of traffic on the shaken ground;
I saw him on the girders where
Men with hammers walled in the air;
And in the awful tunnel built
Through the shifting river silt,
Where gentlemen with polished shoes
Ride at ease and read the news,
Dry and smug, dry and smug,
Far beneath a ferry and tug
That in the fog from off the sea
Pass and whistle mournfully,
There I smelled the steamy breath
Sighing from the lungs of Death.

In the evening I would sit
In my room and think of it,—
Think of fire that suddenly
Licks the wall, and none knows why,
And from the twentieth story hurls
To the pave the factory girls;
Think of ice-bergs rocking slow
Southward from the broken flow,—
Of a sailor on the deep
Roughly shaken out of sleep
By a mountain bright and dim,
Bending green eyes down on him.

*

When I see my netted veins
Blue and busy, while the grains
In the little glass of ME
Tumble to eternity,—
When I feel my body's heat
Surge beneath the icy sheet,
Body that in this same place,
With the sheet across its face,
Turned to ice inscrutably,
Will be lying soon maybe,
In my ear a voice will sigh,
"Here am I—I—I—!"

Bounding up in bed I shriek,
"Who is in this room?—Speak!"
And the clock ticks on the shelf.
And I know that Death himself
Came between the curtains there,
Laid his hand upon a chair,
Caught his image fleetingly
In the glass that mirrors me.

※

Once upon a time I sat
Making verses, while the cat,
Half-asleep against my knee,
Clawed a cushion purringly.
As I watched the moving claws,
Musing wisely on the cause—
Early habit ruling yet
In this droll domestic pet—
Suddenly I was aware
That a Cat, as well, was there,
Through the slits in his round eyes
Watching me without surprise;
Cat, whose purring seemed to say,
"Some day—some day—"

PART FIVE

1

THE SEA at sunset can reflect,
And does, the thin flamingo cloud,
The pale-green rift beneath; the sky
Alone can say these things aloud;
The water ripples, and refracts
Celestial into water acts.
But this is lovely: you detect
The sky, from ocean's brief defect.

I left the island, left the sea,
Heartbroken for the twentieth time,—
"Beauty does not belong to me,"
I said, yet as I said it, knew
That this had never yet been true.
The sea was grey, the sea was blue,
The sea was white and streaked with spume,
Crowded with waves, but still had room
For wreckage; and the sea was green
Bursting against a reef unseen
Until the heavy swell sucked back,
Leaving the reef exposed and black.

In Vermont—and the stars so clear,
Seen through the dustless atmosphere,
That stars ahead both blazed and glowed
Only a foot above the road.
And then remorselessly appeared,
To eyes grown tired of lovely sights,
The flushing, soaring Northern Lights—
And still the eyes and mind must take
More wonder, and remain awake.

And then, again, the gleaming chasm
Began to vibrate, and I knew,
In spite of all that I could do,
I must endure the awful spasm
Of perfectness accomplished, sure
And terrible—so drove my eyes
Into the Northern-lighted skies;
And suffered Beauty to extent
Extreme, and with no merriment.

I sent my mind ahead to climb
The Mohawk Trail: which can be bad
In fog, and fog is what we had
Always; I spread the motor-map,
And left it lying on my lap.

2

I, IN disgust with the living, having read
Much of the accomplished dead,
Was nagged by the clucking of the robin, clucking her
    over-fed
Young off the nest—and what a night, I said,
Raining cats and dogs and blowing like hell,
    To haul babies out of bed.

And I thought: their wings will be wet,
And heavy, in the long grass; and she will not let me
    help her, she is such a fuss-
Budget, and so stupid, trusting the hostile
Weather, and afraid of her friends. Oh, well.

"Afraid of her friends"? . . . I thought of a friendship
    extended to me,
And of my rejecting it, suspicious and wary.
And then I thought of the sea making
Between Ragged and Orr's,
And between their shores four miles of open water, and
    the wind blowing up, and a wicked swell, and me

Pitched and sliding and banged by the wave under
    the bow, and drenched with spray, and snug and
    content . . .
Because I knew that the sea
Was not concerned with me, might possibly
Drown me, but willed me no ill.

3

How DID I bear it—how could I possibly
    as a child,
On my narrow shoulders and pipe-stem legs
    have supported
The fragrance and the colour of the
    frangible hour, the deep
Taste of the shallow dish?—It is not
    as if
I had thought, being a child, that the beautiful
    thing would last: it passed while
    I looked at it,
Except, of course, in memory—memory
    is the seventh
Colour in the spectrum. But I knew about—
    when even then,
The grapevine growing over the grey
    rock—the shock
Of beauty seen, noticed, for the
    first time—
I remember it well—and I remember
    where I stood—on which side
    of the rock.

Already the triangular leaves on the grape-trellis
  are green; they have given me no time
To report their colour as it was when I first
Came upon them, wondering if the strawberry rhubarb
  was up, looking for the pretty, feared
  hoof-marks of deer
In the asparagus.

How did I bear it?—Now—grown up and encased
In the armour of custom, after years
Of looking at loveliness, forewarned
  and face to face, and no time
  and too prudent
At six in the morning to accept the unendurable
  embrace,

I come back from the garden into the kitchen,
  and take off my rubbers—the dew
Is heavy and high, wetting the sock above
  the shoe—but I cannot do
The housework yet.

4

MEN WORKING

CHARMING, THE movement of girls about a May-pole in
    May,
Weaving the coloured ribbons in and out,
Charming; youth is charming, youth is fair.

But beautiful the movement of men striking pikes
Into the end of a black pole, and slowly
Raising it out of the damp grass and up into the air.
The clean strike of the pike into the pole: beautiful.

Joe is the boss; but Ed or Bill will say,
"No, Joe; we can't get it that way—
We've got to take it from here. Are you okay
On your side, Joe?" "Yes," says the boss. "Okay."

The clean strike of the pike into the pole—*"That's it!"*
"Ground your pikes!"

The grounded pikes about the rising black pole,
    beautiful.
"Ed, you'd better get under here with me!" "I'm
Under!"

"That's it!"
"Ground your pikes!"

Joe says, "Now, boys, don't heave
Too hard—we've got her—but you, Ed, you and Mike,
You'll have to hold her from underneath while Bill
Shifts his pike—she wants to fall downhill;
We've got her all right, but we've got her on a slight
Slant."
"That's it!"—"Mike,
About six feet lower this time."
"That's it!"

"Ground your pikes!"

One by one the pikes are moved about the pole, more
      beautiful
Than coloured ribbons weaving.

The clean strike of the pike into the pole; each man
Depending on the skill
And the balance, both of body and of mind,
Of each of the others: in the back of each man's mind
The respect for the pole: it is forty feet high, and weighs
Two thousand pounds.

In the front of each man's mind: "She's going to go
Exactly where we want her to go: this pole
Is going to go into that seven-foot hole we dug
For her
To stand in."

This was in the deepening dusk of a July night.
They were putting in the poles: bringing the electric
    light.

5

STEEPLETOP

1

EVEN YOU, Sweet Basil: even you,
Lemon Verbena: must exert yourselves now
    and somewhat harden
Against untimely frost; I have hovered you and
    covered you and kept going
    smudges,
Until I am close to worn-out. Now, you
Go about it. I have other things to do,
Writing poetry, for instance. And I, too,
Live in this garden.

2

Nothing could stand
All this rain.
The lilacs were drowned, browned
    before I had even
    smelled them
Cool against my cheek, held down
A little by my hand.

Pain
Is seldom preventable, but is
 presentable
Even to strangers on a train—
But what the rain
Does to the lilacs—is something
 you must sigh and try
To explain.

3

Borage, forage for bees
And for those who love blue,
Why must you,
Having only been transplanted
From where you were not wanted
Either by the bee or by me
From under the sage, engage in this
 self-destruction?
I was tender about your slender
 tap-root.
I thought you would send out shoot after
 shoot
Of thick cucumber-smelling, hairy leaves.
But why anybody believes
Anything, I do not know. I thought I
 could trust you.

6

THE GARDENER IN HAYING-TIME

I HAD a gardener. I had him until haying-time.
In haying-time they set him pitching hay.
I had two gardeners. I had them until haying-time.
In haying-time they set them pitching hay.
I had three gardeners. I had them until haying-time.
—Can life go on this way?

7

Sky-coloured bird, blue wings with no more
    spots of spotless white
Dappled, than on a day in spring
When the brown meadows trickle with a hundred
    brooks two inches broad and wink and flash back
    light—
Dappled with no more white than on
    an all but cloudless sky makes
    clear blue deeper and more bright.

Exquisite glutton, azure coward with
    proud crest
And iridescent nape—
Mild milky mauve, chalcedony,
    then lustred, and all amethyst, then brushed with
    bronze, the half-green clustered with the ripe grape,
    under the lapis crest.
Dull-feathered bird today, pecking at ashes by the
    cinder-pit, your clanging tone alone makes known
    our northern jay
Sky-coloured—under a slaty sky sky-coloured
    still, slate-grey.

8

TO A SNAKE

Poor dying thing; it was my dog, not I,
That did for you.
I gave you a wide arc, and moved to pass.

And yet, I was not sad that you should die;
You jarred me so; you were too motionless
And sudden, coiled there in the grass.

Now, you are coiled no longer. Now
Your splendid, streakèd back is to the ground.
Your beautiful, light-scarlet blood is spattered,
And shines in dreadful dew-drops all around.

And that white, ugly belly you had not confessed,—
So naked, so unscrolled with patterns—is at last exposed.

Oh—oh—I do not like to see
A fellow-mortal's final agony!
We shared this world all summer until now!
Now,—off you go.

All upside-down you lie, less looped than flung.
And all but done for.
And yet,—with head still raised; and that red, flickering
tongue.

9

I WOKE in the night and heard the wind, and it blowing
   half a gale.
"Blizzard, by gum!" I said to myself out loud, "What an
   elegant
Hissing and howling, what a roar!"
And I rose, half-rose, in bed, and
Listened to the wind, smelling new snow—
No smell like that—a smell neither sour nor sweet—
No fragrance, none at all, nothing to compete with,
   nothing to interfere
With the odorless clear passage of the smell of new snow
Through the nostrils. "Cold," I said;
And clawed up the extra blanket from the foot of the bed.
Lying there, coiled and cuddled within my own warmth,
Ephemeral but far from frail,
I listened to the winding-up from a sound almost not
   heard, to the yelling hurling
Thump against the house of an all-but-official gale
And thought, "Bad night for a sail
Except far out at sea . . ."

And somewhere something heavy bumped and rolled
And bumped, like a barrel of molasses loose in the hold.

10

Look how the bittersweet with lazy
        muscle moves aside
Great stones placed here by planning
        men not without sweat and pride.
And yet how beautiful this broken
        wall applied
No more to its first duty: to keep
        sheep or cattle in;
Bought up by Beauty now, with the whole
        calm abandoned countryside.

And how the bittersweet to meet the
        stunned admiring eye with all
The red and orange splendour of its fruit
        at the first stare
Unclasps its covering leaves, lets them
        all fall,
Strips to the twig, is bare.

See, too, the nightshade, the woody, the
        bittersweet, strangling the wall

For this, the beauty of berries, this
    scandalous, bright
Persimmon and tangerine comment on
    fieldstone, on granite and on
    quartz, by might
Of men and crowbars, and a rock for
    lever, and a rock above a rock wedged
    in, and the leverage right,
Wrested from the tough acres that in
    time must yield
And suffer plow and harrow
    and be a man's hay-field—
Wrested, hoisted, balanced on its edge,
    tipped, tumbled, clear
Of its smooth-walled cool hole lying,
    dark and damp side upward
    in the sun, inched and urged
    upon the stone-boat, hauled here.

Yet mark where the rowan, the mountain
    ash berries, hang bunched amid leaves
    like ferns,
Scarlet in clear blue air, and the tamarack
    turns
Yellow as mustard, and sheds its short
    needles to lie on the ground like light

Through the door of a hut in the forest
　　to travellers miles off the road at night;
Where brilliant the briony glows in the hedge,
　　frail, clustered, elliptical fruit;
Nightshade conserving in capsules transparent
　　of jacinth and amber its
　　jellies of ill-repute.

And only the cherries, that ripened for robins
　　and cherry-birds, burned
With more ruddy a spark than the bark and
　　the leaves of the cherry-tree,
　　red in October turned.

11

TRUCK-GARDEN MARKET-DAY

PEACEFUL AND slow, peaceful and slow,
Skillful and deft, in my own rhythm,
Happy about the house I go—
For the men are in town, and their noise gone with

Well I remember, long ago,
How still, in my girlish room, the night was—
Watching the moon from my window,
While cool on the empty bed her light was.

More than my heart to him I gave,
When I gave my heart in soft surrender—
Who now am the timid, laughed-at slave
Of a man unaware of this, and tender.

Never must he know how I feel,
Or how, at times, too loud his voice is—
When, just at the creak of his wagon-wheel
Cramped for the barn, my life rejoices!

He would be troubled; he could not learn
How small a part of myself I keep
To smell the meadows, or sun the churn,
When he's at market, or while he's asleep.

INTENSE AND terrible, I think, must be the loneliness
Of infants—look at all
The Teddy-bears clasped in slumber in slatted cribs
Painted pale-blue or pink.
And all the Easter Bunnies, dirty and disreputable, that
    deface
The white pillow and the sterile, immaculate, sunny,
    turning pleasantly in space,
Dainty abode of Baby—try to replace them
With new ones, come Easter again, fluffy and white, and
    with a different smell;
Release with gentle force from the horrified embrace,
That hugs until the stitches give and the stuffing shows,
His only link with a life of his own, the only thing he
    really knows . . .
Try to sneak it out of sight.
If you wish to hear anger yell glorious
From air-filled lungs through a throat unthrottled
By what the neighbours will say;
If you wish to witness a human countenance contorted
And convulsed and crumpled by helpless grief and
    despair,

Then stand beside the slatted crib and say There, there,
    and take the toy away.

Pink and pale-blue look well
In a nursery. And for the most part Baby is really good:
He gurgles, he whimpers, he tries to get his toe to his
    mouth; he slobbers his food
Dreamily—cereals and vegetable juices—onto his bib:
He behaves as he should.

But do not for a moment believe he has forgotten Black-
    ness; nor the deep
Easy swell; nor his thwarted
Design to remain for ever there;
Nor the crimson betrayal of his birth into a yellow glare.
The pictures painted on the inner eyelids of infants just
    before they sleep,
Are not in pastel.

Sometimes, oh, often, indeed, in the midst of ugly
    adversity, beautiful
Memories return.
You awake in wonder, you awake at half-past four,
Wondering what wonder is in store.
You reach for your clothes in the dark and pull them on,
    you have no time
Even to wash your face, you have to climb Megunticook.

You run through the sleeping town; you do not arouse
Even a dog, you are so young and so light on your feet.
What a way to live, what a way . . .
No breakfast, not even hungry. An apple, though,
In the pocket.
And the only people you meet are store-windows.

The path up the mountain is stony and in places steep,
And here it is really dark—wonderful, wonderful,
Wonderful—the smell of bark
And rotten leaves and dew! And nobody awake
In all the world but you!—
Who lie on a high cliff until your elbows ache,
To see the sun come up over Penobscot Bay.

14

NOT FOR A NATION

Not for a nation:
Not the dividing, the estranging, thing
For;
Nor, in a world so small, the insulation
Of dream from dream—where dreams are links in
    the chain
Of a common hope; that man may yet regain
His dignity on earth—where before all
Eyes: small eyes of elephant and shark; still
Eyes of lizard grey in the sub-tropic noon,
Blowing his throat out into a scarlet, edged-with-cream
    incredible balloon
Suddenly, and suddenly dancing, hoisting and lowering
    his body on his short legs on the hot
    stone window-sill;
And the eyes of the upturned, grooved and dusty,
    rounded, dull cut-worm
Staring upward at the spade,—
These, all these, and more, from the corner of the eye
    see man, infirm,
Tottering like a tree about to fall,—

Who yet had such high dreams—who not for this was
    made (or so said he),—nor did design to die
    at all.

*

Not for a nation,
Not the dividing, the estranging thing
For;
Nor, on a world so small, the insulation
Of dream from dream,
In what might be today, had we been better welders,
    a new chain for pulling down old buildings,
    uprooting the wrong trees; these
Not for;
Not for my country right or wrong;
Not for the drum or the bugle; not for the song
Which pipes me away from my home against my will
    along with the other children
To where I would not go
And makes me say what I promised never to say,
    and do the thing I am through with—
Into the Piper's Hill;
Not for the flag
Of any land because myself was born there
Will I give up my life.

But I will love that land where man is free,
And that will I defend.
"To the end?" you ask, "To the end?"—Naturally,
  to the end.

*

What is it to the world, or to me,
That I beneath an elm, not beneath a tamarisk-tree
First filled my lungs, and clenched my tiny hands already
  spurred and nailed
Against the world, and wailed
In anger and frustration that all my tricks had failed and
  I been torn
Out of the cave where I was hiding, to suffer in the
  world as I have done and I still do—
Never again—oh, no, no more on earth—ever again to
  find abiding-place.
Birth—awful birth . . .
Whatever the country, whatever the colour and race.

*

The colour and the traits of each,
The shaping of his speech,—
These can the elm, given a long time, alter; these,
Too, the tamarisk.

But if he starve, but if he freeze—
Early, in his own tongue, he knows;
And though with arms or bows or a dipped thorn
Blown through a tube, he fights—the brisk
Rattle of shot he is not slow to tell
From the sound of ripe seed bursting from a poddy shell;
And he whom, all his life, life has abused
Yet knows if he be justly or unjustly used.

*

I know these elms, this beautiful doorway: here
I am at home, if anywhere.
A natural fondness, an affection which need never be
    said,
Rises from the wooden sidewalks warm as the smell of
    new-baked bread
From a neighbour's kitchen. It is dusk. The sun goes
    down.
Sparsely strung along the street the thrifty lights appear.
It is pleasant. It is good.
I am very well-known here; here I am understood.
I can walk along the street, or turn into a path unlighted,
    without fear
Of poisonous snakes, or of any face in town.
Tall elms, my roots go down
As deep as yours into this soil, yes, quite as deep.
And I hear the rocking of my cradle. And I must not
    sleep.

*

Not for a nation; not for a little town,
Where, when the sun goes down, you may sit without
    fear
On the front porch, just out of reach of the arc-light,
    rocking,
With supper ready, wearing a pale new dress, and your
    baby near
In its crib, and your husband due to be home by the next
    trolley that you hear bumping into Elm Street—
    no:
But for a dream that was dreamt an elm-tree's life ago—
And longer, yes, much longer, and what I mean you
    know.

For the dream, for the plan, for the freedom of man as
    it was meant
To be;
Not for the structure set up so lustily, by rule of thumb
And over-night, bound to become
Loose, lop-sided, out of plumb,
But for the dream, for the plan, for the freedom of man
    as it was meant
To be
By men with more vision, more wisdom, more purpose,
    more brains
Than we,
(Possibly, possibly)

Men with more courage, men more unselfish, more
    intent
Than we, upon their dreams, upon their dream of Free-
    dom,—Freedom not alone
For oneself, but for all, wherever the word is known,
In whatever tongue, or the longing in whatever spirit—
Men with more honor. (That remains
To be seen! That we shall see!)

Possibly. Possibly.

And if still these truths be held to be
Self-evident.

PART SIX

Sonnets

1

Those hours when happy hours were my estate,—
Entailed, as proper, for the next in line,
Yet mine the harvest, and the title mine—
Those acres, fertile, and the furrow straight,
From which the lark would rise—all of my late
Enchantments, still, in brilliant colours, shine,
But striped with black, the tulip, lawn and vine,
Like gardens looked at through an iron gate.

Yet not as one who never sojourned there
I view the lovely segments of a past
I lived with all my senses, well aware
That this was perfect, and it would not last:
I smell the flower, though vacuum-still the air;
I feel its texture, though the gate is fast.

Not, to me, less lavish—though my dreams have been
    splendid—
Than dreams, have been the hours of the actual day:
Never, awaking, did I awake to say:
"Nothing could be like that," when a dream was ended.
Colours, in dream; ecstasy, in dream extended
Beyond the edge of sleep—these, in their way,
Approach, come even close, yet pause, yet stay,
In the high presence of request by its answer attended.

Music, and painting, poetry, love, and grief,
Had they been more intense, I could not have borne,—
Yet, not, I think, through stout endurance lacked;
Rather, because the budding and the falling leaf
Were one, and wonderful,—not to be torn
Apart: I ask of dream: seem like the fact.

Tranquility at length, when autumn comes,
Will lie upon the spirit like that haze
Touching far islands on fine autumn days
With tenderest blue, like bloom on purple plums;
Harvest will ring, but not as summer hums,
With noisy enterprise—to broaden, raise,
Proceed, proclaim, establish: autumn stays
The marching year one moment; stills the drums.

Then sits the insistent cricket in the grass;
But on the gravel crawls the chilly bee;
And all is over that could come to pass
Last year; excepting this: the mind is free
One moment, to compute, refute, amass,
Catalogue, question, contemplate, and see.

4

SONNET IN DIALECTIC

AND IS indeed truth beauty?—at the cost
Of all else that we cared for, can this be?—
To see the coarse triumphant, and to see
Honour and pity ridiculed, and tossed
Upon a poked-at fire; all courage lost
Save what is whelped and fattened by decree
To move among the unsuspecting free
And trap the thoughtful, with their thoughts engrossed?

Drag yet that stream for Beauty, if you will;
And find her, if you can; finding her drowned
Will not dismay your ethics,—you will still
To one and all insist she has been found . . .
And haggard men will smile your praise, until,
Some day, they stumble on her burial-mound.

5

To HOLD secure the province of Pure Art,—
What if the crude and weighty task were mine?—
For him who runs, cutting the pen less fine
Than formerly, and in the indignant heart
Dipping it straight? (to issue thence a dart,
And shine no more except as weapons shine)
The deeply-loved, the laboured, polished line
Eschew for ever?—this to be my part?

Attacked that Temple is which must not fall—
Under whose ancient shade Calliope,
Thalia, Euterpe, the nine Muses all
Went once about their happy business free:
Could I but write the Writing on the Wall!—
What matter, if one poet cease to be.

6

And if I die, because that part of me
Which part alone of me had chance to live,
Chose to be honour's threshing-floor, a sieve
Where right through wrong might make its way, and be;
If from all taint of indignation, free
Must be my art, and thereby fugitive
From all that threatens it—why—let me give
To moles my dubious immortality.

For, should I cancel by one passionate screed
All that in chaste reflection I have writ,
So that again not ever in bright need
A man shall want my verse and reach for it,
I and my verses will be dead indeed,—
That which we died to champion, hurt no whit.

It is the fashion now to wave aside
As tedious, obvious, vacuous, trivial, trite,
All things which do not tickle, tease, excite
To some subversion, or in verbiage hide
Intent, or mock, or with hot sauce provide
A dish to prick the thickened appetite;
Straightforwardness is wrong, evasion right;
It is correct, *de rigueur,* to deride.

What fumy wits these modern wags expose,
For all their versatility: Voltaire,
Who wore to bed a night-cap, and would close,
In fear of drafts, all windows, could declare
In antique stuffiness, a phrase that blows
Still through men's smoky minds, and clears the air.

8

Alcestis to her husband, just before,
with his tearful approbation, she dies
in order that he may live.

Admetus, from my marrow's core I do
Despise you: wherefore pity not your wife,
Who, having seen expire her love for you
With heaviest grief, today gives up her life.
You could not with your mind imagine this:
One might surrender, yet continue proud.
Not having loved, you do not know: the kiss
You sadly beg, is impious, not allowed.

Of all I loved,—how many girls and men
Have loved me in return?—speak!—young or old—
Speak!—sleek or famished, can you find me then
One form would flank me, as this night grows cold?
I am at peace, Admetus—go and slake
Your grief with wine. I die for my own sake.

9

WHAT CHORES these churls do put upon the great,
What chains, what harness; the unfettered mind,
At dawn, in all directions flying blind
Yet certain, might accomplish, might create
What all men must consult or contemplate,—
Save that the spirit, earth-born and born kind,
Cannot forget small questions left behind,
Nor honest human impulse underrate:
Oh, how the speaking pen has been impeded,
To its own cost and to the cost of speech,
By specious hands that for some thinly-needed
Answer or autograph, would claw a breach
In perfect thought . . . till broken thought receded
And ebbed in foam, like ocean down a beach.

I WILL put Chaos into fourteen lines
And keep him there; and let him thence escape
If he be lucky; let him twist, and ape
Flood, fire, and demon—his adroit designs
Will strain to nothing in the strict confines
Of this sweet Order, where, in pious rape,
I hold his essence and amorphous shape,
Till he with Order mingles and combines.
Past are the hours, the years, of our duress,
His arrogance, our awful servitude:
I have him. He is nothing more nor less
Than something simple not yet understood;
I shall not even force him to confess;
Or answer. I will only make him good.

COME HOME, victorious wounded!—let the dead,
The out-of-it, the more victorious still,
Hold in the cold the hot-contested hill,
Hold by the sand the abandoned smooth beach-head;—
Maimed men, whose scars must be exhibited
To all the world, though much against your will—
And men whose bodies bear no marks of ill,
Being twisted only in the guts and head:
Come home! come home!—not to the home you long
To find,—and which your valour had achieved
Had virtue been but right, and evil wrong!—
We have tried hard, and we have greatly grieved:
Come home and help us!—you are hurt but strong!
—And we—we are bewildered—and bereaved.

12

READ HISTORY: so learn your place in Time;
And go to sleep: all this was done before;
We do it better, fouling every shore;
We disinfect, we do not probe, the crime.
Our engines plunge into the seas, they climb
Above our atmosphere: we grow not more
Profound as we approach the ocean's floor;
Our flight is lofty, it is not sublime.

Yet long ago this Earth by struggling men
Was scuffed, was scraped by mouths that bubbled mud;
And will be so again, and yet again;
Until we trace our poison to its bud
And root, and there uproot it: until then,
Earth will be warmed each winter by man's blood.

13

Read history: thus learn how small a space
You may inhabit, nor inhabit long
In crowding Cosmos—in that confined place
Work boldly; build your flimsy barriers strong;
Turn round and round, make warm your nest; among
The other hunting beasts, keep heart and face,—
Not to betray the doomed and splendid race
You are so proud of, to which you belong.

For trouble comes to all of us: the rat
Has courage, in adversity, to fight;
But what a shining animal is man,
Who knows, when pain subsides, that is not that,
For worse than that must follow—yet can write
Music; can laugh; play tennis; even plan.

14

My words that once were virtuous and expressed
Nearly enough the mortal joys I knew,
Now that I sit to supper with the blest
Come haltingly, are very poor and few.
Whereof you speak and wherefore the bright walls
Resound with silver mirth I am aware,
But I am faint beneath the coronals
Of living vines you set upon my hair.

Angelic friends that stand with pointed wings
Sweetly demanding, in what dulcet tone,
How fare I in this heaven of happy things,—
I cannot lift my words against your own.
Forgive the downcast look, the lyre unstrung;
Breathing your presence, I forget your tongue.

15

Now sirs the autumn cricket in the grass,
And on the gravel crawls the chilly bee;
Near to its close and none too soon for me
Draws the dull year, in which has come to pass
The changing of the happy child I was
Into this quiet creature people see
Stitching a seam with careful industry
To deaden you, who died on Michaelmas.

Ages ago the purple aconite
Laid its dark hoods about it on the ground,
And roses budded small and were content;
Swallows are south long since and out of sight;
With you the phlox and asters also went;
Nor can my laughter anywhere be found.

AND MUST I then, indeed, Pain, live with you
All through my life?—sharing my fire, my bed,
Sharing—oh, worst of all things!—the same head?—
And, when I feed myself, feeding you, too?
So be it, then, if what seems true, is true:
Let us to dinner, comrade, and be fed;—
I cannot die till you yourself are dead,
And, with you living, I can live life through.

Yet have you done me harm, ungracious guest,
Spying upon my ardent offices
With frosty look; robbing my nights of rest;
And making harder things I did with ease.
You will die with me: but I shall, at best,
Forgive you with restraint, for deeds like these.

17

IF I die solvent—die, that is to say,
In full possession of my critical mind,
Not having cast, to keep the wolves at bay
In this dark wood—till all be flung behind—
Wit, courage, honour, pride, oblivion
Of the red eyeball and the yellow tooth;
Nor sweat nor howl nor break into a run
When loping Death's upon me in hot sooth;
'Twill be that in my honoured hands I bear
What's under no condition to be spilled
Till my blood spills and hardens in the air:
An earthen grail, a humble vessel filled
To its low brim with water from that brink
Where Shakespeare, Keats and Chaucer learned to drink.

GRIEF THAT is grief and properly so hight
Has lodging in the orphaned brain alone,
Whose nest is cold, whose wings are now his own
And thinly feathered for the perchless flight
Between the owl and ermine; overnight
His food is reason, fodder for the grown,
His range is north to famine, south to fright.
When Constant Care was manna to the beak,
And Love Triumphant downed the hovering breast,
Vainly the cuckoo's child might nudge and speak
In ugly whispers to the indignant nest:
How even a feathered heart had power to break,
And thud no more above their huddled rest.

Felicity of Grief!—even Death being kind,
Reminding us how much we dared to love!
There, once, the challenge lay,—like a light glove
Dropped as through carelessness—easy to find
Means and excuse for being somewhat blind
Just at that moment; and why bend above,
Take up, such certain anguish for the mind?
Ah, you who suffer now as I now do,
Seeing, of Life's dimensions, not one left
Save Time—long days somehow to be lived through:
Think—of how great a thing were you bereft
That it should weigh so now!—and that you knew
Always, its awkward contours, and its heft.

20

WHAT RIDER spurs him from the darkening east
As from a forest, and with rapid pound
Of hooves, now light, now louder on hard ground,
Approaches, and rides past with speed increased,
Dark spots and flecks of foam upon his beast?
What shouts he from the saddle, turning 'round,
As he rides on?—"Greetings!"—I made the sound;
"Greetings from Ninevah!"—it seemed, at least.

Did someone catch the object that he flung?
He held some object on his saddle-bow,
And flung it towards us as he passed; among
The children then it fell most likely; no,
'Tis here: a little bell without a tongue.
Listen; it has a faint voice even so.

Set in Linotype Fairfield
Format by Robert Cheney
Manufactured by The Haddon Craftsmen, Inc.
Published by HARPER & BROTHERS, New York